LET'S TALK

LET'S TALK

Communicating with Today's Youth

Dr. Kimberly N. Jackson

Library of Congress Cataloging-in-Publication Data
Jackson, Kimberly,
ISBN: 979-8-218-65475-7

DEDICATION

I dedicate this book to all the misunderstood kids and parents searching for a connection. It really is possible . . .

TABLE OF CONTENTS

Acknowledgments. ix

Introduction. xi

The Maturity Gap and Communication 1

The Foundations of Emotional Intelligence and Communication 4

Factors and Influences on Communication 6

Nonverbal Communication. 10

Navigating Modern Communication Challenges 12

Creating a Safe Space 15

When Communication Breaks Down 23

Research-Based Suggestions for Effective, Healthy Communication 27

Conclusion: Let's Talk—and Keep Talking 39

References. 41

Discussion Questions 44

Activities to Support Improved Communication 45

ACKNOWLEDGMENTS

I would like to acknowledge the positive forces in my life that encourage me to write. Anissa Burdett has continued to be my accountability partner who simply won't let me stop. Her belief in me has at times been the only thing that has kept the words flowing. Thank you to Uncle Mike and Aunt Evelyn for their thoughtful prayers as I finalized this writing.

This book is inspired by all the young people that I've been blessed to encounter in life, and the ongoing struggle that I've both experienced and witnessed in effectively communicating with them. I've had the opportunity to serve as the principal of various schools ranging from kindergarten through high school, and I have also had the pleasure of coaching young people at some of the highest levels of athletic competition. In each of these experiences, I see and feel the pain and struggle that exists in the communication between the youth I encounter and the adults in their lives. What I've learned is that the barriers that exist in communication create relationship barriers that often impede so many other critical areas and opportunities.

I was blessed with an opportunity to step outside of my comfort zone. As one of the few females in my age group growing up, and the mother of three young men, working with boys was my primary experience, until I began coaching basketball. I inherited a team where I was surrounded by an amazing group of young ladies who taught me how to both talk to and listen to young people differently. I will be forever grateful.

I took over the basketball team when the girls were in middle school, and we stayed together until they were sophomores in high school. These girls became family to me, and I believe they saw me as a big sister, for some even a mother figure. They were from various walks of life with all different needs, yet they all had a common gift, they were all amazing athletes with beautiful souls! We traveled around the country, mainly by car, and the conversations that we had together opened my eyes to both the desire and need for our young people to have a trusted person to talk to about all the things running through their minds and hearts. I'll admit that there were road trips where all I wanted to do was escape the car, but through each adventure, I was grateful for the experience. These girls trusted me, and in return, I gave them truthful and open dialogue in a way that I had not in the past with other youth. Again, they taught me how to first listen, then they helped me learn how to effectively communicate through a foundation of trust.

I talked to these young ladies about everything from grades to relationships and sex. They asked me anything that came to mind and learned to trust that I would give them my best and most honest answer to what they asked. This included saying, "I don't know," when their question was beyond my knowledge, followed up with "We can find out together," so they could still have even the hardest question(s) answered. You wouldn't believe the things that kids are curious about when you simply allow them to ask without judgment. We expressed our frustrations and fears and learned to encourage each other in both our victories and defeats. We all grew and learned during our precious time together. With each conversation, I was proud of the truthful and healthy dialogue knowing that everyone involved was gaining in the experience. Although we were together because of basketball, it was the least of where we all found benefit in the relationship, it was simply our excuse to be.

To this day I still communicate with some of these young ladies who are now in their late twenties to early thirties and still blazing trails of adventure and success in life. I'm both grateful and proud to have been their coach because what I gained from them far surpasses anything I ever had to offer back. These ladies taught me the language of our young people in both heart and mind, and I give them a great deal of credit for my ability to successfully navigate that communication now. Ladies of the Jets, Lou-E-Ville Elite, St. Louis Adidas, and Midwest Elite, you will forever be my greatest teachers in life, love, and relationship. Thank you for allowing me to be a part of the greatness that each of you have and will become, and I am so proud of each of you . . . "my ladies."

INTRODUCTION

I have served as a principal of urban schools where the constant noise of lockers and laughter is a familiar sound. Within this role, I find myself being a mentor, and sometimes, a much-needed ally. Over the years, the challenge of leading schools has become more and more complicated. Each environment presents itself as just as much of a test as the next. The biggest thing that stands out is the essential need for genuine connection.

I've seen situations where the lives of the young people I work with resemble battlegrounds, with students facing daily challenges far beyond just academic struggles. These young people often navigate violence, behavioral issues, and tensions that stem from deep-seated trauma and sometimes neglect. These types of challenges can deter the opportunities for future success that should be achievable for every student.

Building connections with some of these students involves more than just understanding them; it requires us to step into their experiences, which is often more difficult than we might anticipate. This work is critical and it's about building bridges over troubled waters and sometimes offering safe passage for those who've only known and felt the hardships of the storm. By modeling empathy and fostering genuine dialogue, I've not only been able to connect with many of the young people around me, but I have also been able to coach others through how to engage effectively.

Consider my son's transition to middle school, a time filled with uncertainty that could have easily led to ongoing turmoil. Middle school can feel like a new world with each day presenting new challenges. Through open, consistent, and sometimes creative conversations, what could have been a stressful time (and absolutely was at times) turned into an opportunity for self-advocacy and growth. My son's successful navigation of this transition is a testament to the power of effective communication. It transformed potential problems into opportunities for growth.

Barriers in communication take on different faces. Many people see the barriers of communication as a dynamic of language or dialect, but it's so much deeper. The way that each of us speaks, hears, and thinks creates different understandings and definitions for the words and situations around us. How we speak and how we hear are personal; it's learned behavior that's built on influences and beliefs beyond our conscious understanding. This is true for people of all ages and creates the stage for the struggles that exist in effective communication between the young and old. It's my belief that as an adult, the ownership of repairing this communication failure, as it relates to our youth, falls on me and the other adults within the lives of our young people. We simply have to do better.

I have regular interaction with the parents of students within the school where I am the principal. The number one struggle that I see is the inability of adults to break through the walls that our young people have built and open up genuine lines of communication that will allow parents and other adults to understand and assist with students' needs. Everything from the lingo that's used to their experiences in today's fast-paced digital world feels foreign to us. The goal of this book is to open a dialogue among those of us facing this challenge that will assist each of us in finding success.

How do we as the adults who have been charged with the support of these young people put our best foot forward toward understanding and helping them? With the minimal communication that some of our young people offer, how do we even know what they need?

When parents approach me with these types of questions or when I struggle with these concerns with my own kids, I always try to go back and remember what it was like being a young person myself. I remember how hard it was to talk to adults and feel confident at times to open my mouth and say what was on my mind. I then ask myself why it was like that, and I remember feeling as though I was alone in my concerns and uncertain of how the adults around me would respond. I felt insecure about how I would be viewed for the things that I was thinking so I found it better to just keep them to myself. I remember feeling that I would be judged for my thoughts and questions, and I felt afraid and ashamed. This wasn't because the response that I was getting from adults always reinforced these beliefs, but rather because as a young person I lacked the experience and confidence to know what was normal and what wasn't. Whether we want to acknowledge it or not, kids have very complicated and legitimate thoughts and concerns just as we adults do, and as they grow and learn, they need a nonjudgmental outlet of acceptance to discuss what they are thinking.

So how do we bridge that gap of understanding and comfort between adults and young people to open the lines for better communication? How do we create and facilitate that comfort and confidence within our young people to say the things that they feel to us so we can process these feelings and emotions with them before they make their decisions? There is no simple step-by-step answer outside of creating environments that are accepting and normalize the experiences of our youth. This means opening the lines of communication with our youth in creative ways that lay the groundwork of comfort and safety for discussions around any topic.

When I observe many of the relationships that adults have with the teenagers around me, it is painfully obvious that one of the biggest issues in our communication is the perceived negative message that youth tend to hear. How we mean it and what they hear don't match because we don't speak or hear the same language. We mean it in love, and they take it as an indication of their failure. The question then becomes how do we bridge that language gap?

How many conversations do we have with our kids around normal things that are related to their interests in contrast to those related to giving them directions, directives, and correction? For almost everyone reading, the proportion that you come up with in an honest assessment of your interactions will likely correlate with your success in communicating with your child. The parents I've encountered who regularly talk to their kids about topics of interest rather than directive conversations traditionally have better relationships with their kids. This seems like common sense, but going back to what we mean versus what they hear, it's a lot harder than at first glance. We desperately need to learn to speak as they hear so that they can accept our message; I didn't say we need to learn to speak like them, I said we need to learn to speak how they hear. We have to challenge ourselves to put our feet in their shoes and utilize our understanding of who they are as well as remember what it felt like to be a kid to help solve the mysteries of what is going through their minds. Then, we have to proactively open the door to those topics. We have to build the confidence within our young people that our motive is in fact love no matter how our message feels at times, while also working to use words of connection and understanding in our communication that helps our conversations seed and grow.

As complicated as this may sound, a great deal of research has been done to help us improve communication. There are several mindful factors that have been identified that will either help or hurt the cause. Understanding how emotions and nonverbal cues play a role in how we communicate are just two examples of how simple awareness can have a significant impact. This book will look at a variety of research-based factors that impact the effectiveness of our communication with the hope that as we know better, we do better.

This book explores how to reach out and truly connect with those who might feel unreachable, turning disconnected relationships and conversations into dialogues that resonate and transform lives. It's about making every interaction count, bridging generational gaps, and building futures where every young person can not only succeed but also thrive.

As you begin your journey toward better communication with the young people in your life, please keep an open mind to the real work it takes, the willingness to change. I was inspired to do this so I could have a better relationship with all the young people that I have been blessed to encounter, but more specifically to have a better relationship with my own kids. As parents, we often talk to our kids, or better yet talk at them, but never really hear what they're saying to us. In that same light, although they hear our words, they often don't hear our message. My journey has helped me to both hear more clearly so I can understand, as well as speak differently so I can be heard. I hope that this book helps you do the same.

THE MATURITY GAP AND COMMUNICATION

Between young people's growing desire for independence and the constant evolution of how we communicate, trying to understand what's going through their minds is like navigating a maze that rearranges itself every few minutes. Depending on their age and emotional maturity, interacting with young people can feel like talking to a completely different person from one day to the next. Some days, they seem to like us, on other days, well, let's just say we've all learned when to take the hint and retreat. No matter what we say or do, cracking the code to their thoughts can feel impossible. Most adults can relate to this when thinking about the young people in their lives, but here's a plot twist: Our kids feel the same way about us.

One of the most common conversations I have is about the maturity of young people, or more accurately, the lack of maturity that many of them possess. Early in my career, I thought the solution was to help students grow up faster. Spoiler alert: That didn't work. The reality is we all mature at our own pace, and it's shaped by a range of factors. We can't slap an age label on developmental milestones and expect it to apply universally. That's in fact one of the biggest shortcomings of our public school system, but that's a topic for another book.

Research has helped us understand general developmental trends, but the traditional characteristics we learned in Psychology 101 are becoming increasingly unreliable (Santrock, 2021). The typical behaviors associated with a given age now seem to have a margin of error of about ±3 years in both physical and emotional development. That might not sound like much, but in terms of a child's emotional and communication skills, it's huge. This means a twelve-year-old entering seventh grade could function emotionally anywhere from a typical nine-year-old to a fifteen-year-old. That's a staggering range of needs to address. So, what's happening?

After years of working with young people, I'm convinced that the hardest thing we ever do in life is grow up. This realization hit me when I truly understood what maturity means. Adulthood and maturity are not the same thing, and maturity isn't just a function of age; it's a combination of emotional, physical, mental, and social growth. These elements develop at different rates, which means a person could be twenty-five physically, seventeen mentally, and twelve emotionally, but all we see is their fully grown exterior.

The Link Between Maturity and Communication

How does all of this connect to communication? At what age do most people fully mature into adulthood, meaning they have enough self-awareness and understanding of the world to function independently while also listening and communicating effectively? Truth? There are plenty of adults who haven't even made it there yet. If we define adulthood by emotional intelligence and communication skills, then let's be honest, some may never reach the standard.

From my observations, most people don't reach this level of maturity until their mid-to-late twenties, when their emotional, mental, and physical development finally catch up with one another (Arnett, 2015). In previous generations, young people may have seemed more mature, but that was often a result of necessity rather than true readiness. When survival depended on working the land, contributing to the household, or preparing for war, people didn't have the luxury of delaying adulthood. In contrast, most of our young people don't carry that same level of responsibility for basic needs today, and I believe that this has slowed down the maturation process.

Over the past few years, I've paid close attention to both the emotional and physical development of students. In middle school, kids come in all shapes and sizes, but I've noticed an increase in those who have not hit typical growth spurts or developmental milestones. This could actually be a positive sign. With healthier diets and more awareness about the dangers of processed foods, kids are consuming fewer artificial growth hormones. This might explain why physical development appears to be occurring at a more natural, gradual pace for many of our young people. While slower physical development might not be a problem, the delayed emotional and social development we're seeing is a different story. When we look at this dynamic, could the cause be a lack of opportunity for genuine self-discovery?

Rethinking the Path to Adulthood

Take a step back and consider the typical journey of a young person from birth to age eighteen. In spite of all the differences we see in people, the overall path of childhood to adulthood is relatively standardized. Between home and school, there are clear expectations, schedules, and routines. Within this structured system, where are the real opportunities for self-discovery? The traditional factory-model education system is designed to churn out students with the same knowledge and skill set, but the world they are entering looks nothing like the world of the past when the factory was built.

Let's get real for a second. Can you imagine the average eighteen-year-old today being drafted to fight in a war? Back in the Vietnam era and earlier, that was reality. Today, we hesitate to send our eighteen-year-olds off to college without a check-in plan, let alone to a battlefield. Maybe it's time we reconsider what we define as adulthood. Who decided eighteen was the magic number? It was probably some parent who couldn't figure out how to manage their child and needed a way to release their responsibility. Joking aside, this artificial assignment of adult age came through necessity, and the reality is, we just don't need them to grow up that fast anymore.

If we want to close the maturity gap, we need to be intentional about how we guide young people toward adulthood. This means adjusting our communication styles, creating real-world learning experiences, and providing structured opportunities for independence. Instead of assuming young people will "just figure it out," we need to meet them where they are developmentally and help them grow. What's the key to making this happen? It's a focus on patience, structure, and a shift in mindset, one that embraces growth over expectation.

The Emotional Roller Coaster of Adolescence

Adolescence is an emotional roller coaster, a time when hormones rage, moods shift unpredictably, and *"I'm fine"* almost never means "I'm fine." The emotional development that occurs during this phase has a significant impact on long-term behavior and decision-making. Ironically, this is also when young people seem the least interested in adult guidance. As frustrating as it may be, we have to remember that we too were once moody, misunderstood teenagers. Our patience and understanding during this stage are absolutely critical. The more we acknowledge and support their emotional needs and respond to the need for understanding of their levels of maturity, the better equipped we are to guide them through this period with minimal damage to their egos and our sanity.

THE FOUNDATIONS OF EMOTIONAL INTELLIGENCE AND COMMUNICATION

Understanding emotions is the key to building meaningful connections and fostering positive relationships, not just within educational settings but across all areas of life. Effective communication isn't just about what we say, it's about how we say it and, more importantly, how we listen. Emotional intelligence (EI) is critical in this process; it helps us establish trust, empathy, and rapport.

EI is defined as the ability to recognize, understand, and manage not only our own emotions but also those of others. Research shows that people with high levels of EI are traditionally more effective communicators and build stronger relationships than those with lower levels of EI (Goleman, 1995).

Emotional Intelligence and Empathy

Recognizing and managing our own emotions, and understanding those of the people we interact with, are foundational skills for effective communication. Self-awareness, a critical element of EI, involves a clear understanding of our strengths, weaknesses, emotions, and the influences they have on our actions and decisions (Goleman, 1995). Being able to see things from another person's perspective is a game-changer in conflict resolution. When people feel heard, they're less likely to escalate the conflict.

Empathy extends beyond simply understanding another's feelings; it involves actively engaging and responding to these emotions in a supportive and compassionate way. This type of engagement is important toward building trust and openness that can enhance personal and professional relationships.

Emotional Regulation: Controlling the Controllable

Emotional regulation refers to our ability to manage and respond to our emotions appropriately. This skill is vital for maintaining composure in

4

challenging situations and expressing emotions in a way that produces positive outcomes. Psychology research shows that emotional regulation is not just about controlling negative emotions but also involves the regulation of positive emotions to fit the appropriateness of various situations (Gross, 1998).

Emotional regulation involves several pieces, including cognitive reappraisal and emotional suppression. Cognitive reappraisal is the process of changing your emotional response to a situation by controlling how you interpret the situation. This technique has been especially effective in reducing the intensity of negative emotions and is associated with better psychological well-being (Gross & John, 2003). In a nutshell, emotional suppression is attempting to control the outward signs of internal emotions.

Effective emotional regulation has significant benefits in personal relationships and professional environments. It gives people the ability to respond to stressors and interpersonal conflicts in a way that preserves the peace and encourages understanding. For example, studies have shown that individuals who excel at emotional regulation are better able to maintain stable and satisfying relationships (Gross, J.J., 1998).

In the workplace and in schools, the ability to regulate emotions contributes to better performance and leadership. Individuals who are good with emotional regulation are more likely to create a positive atmosphere that can enhance team productivity and morale (George, 2000).

The ability to effectively manage emotions has also been linked to physical health benefits. Research shows that poor emotional regulation skills are associated with various health issues, including heart disease, diabetes, and mental health disorders such as depression and anxiety (Chapman et al., 2007).

Emotional regulation is an important aspect of emotional intelligence that impacts almost every area of life. By developing and refining this skill, people can achieve better interpersonal relationships, enhanced professional success, and improved physical and mental health. The ability to regulate our emotions according to the demands of our environment is a powerful tool for managing the complexities of modern life.

Conclusion

Incorporating emotional intelligence into the regular considerations within our daily communications isn't just beneficial, it's essential for developing environments where individuals, especially our young people, can thrive. By investing in our emotional well-being and developing strong EI skills, we improve our ability to connect with others, resolve conflicts more amicably, and build lasting, positive relationships in all areas of life.

FACTORS AND INFLUENCES ON COMMUNICATION

Communication with today's youth is like navigating a new language, one influenced by culture, technology, and generational differences. As society evolves, so do the ways young people express themselves and interpret the world around them. Adults have to recognize how cultural backgrounds and generational trends influence communication styles in order to build meaningful connections.

One of the most significant factors that influences communication with youth is their cognitive development. Research has shown that adolescents process emotions and uncertainty more intensely than adults due to their level of brain development (Steinberg, 2014). Their prefrontal cortex, the part of the brain responsible for decision-making and impulse control, is still developing, while their amygdala, the part of the brain that processes emotions, is very active. The results of this dynamic is that they often overanalyze messages, misinterpret neutral tones as negative, and react impulsively before fully considering the meaning behind a conversation. Recognizing this stage of brain development can help adults approach discussions with more patience and clarity.

The Ear of Our Youth: How They Hear Us

Bill and Pam Farrel's book *Men Are Like Waffles, Women Are Like Spaghetti* offers a helpful analogy in understanding the communication gap that exists between adults and young people: we may speak in one "color" but hear in another (Farrel & Farrel, 2017). This concept applies directly to our communication with our youth. Young people process messages through a variety of ever-changing filters, influenced by emotions, social pressures, and cognitive development.

A message delivered one day may be received entirely differently the next, depending on their mood, stress levels, or peer influence. Adults also bring their own biases to the table that can misinterpret how we perceive youth responses. The challenge is not just to speak clearly, but to understand how messages are being heard and processed for understanding. Cultural context plays a significant role in shaping how youth interpret messages.

The Impact of Culture

Culture can significantly impact how messages are received. Young people from immigrant families, multicultural communities, or diverse upbringings bring diverse perspectives that influence how they communicate. According to Ting-Toomey and Dorjee (2018), communication norms vary widely across different backgrounds, and what's considered respectful in one culture may not hold the same meaning in another. For example, some young people may have been raised to view direct eye contact as a sign of confidence, while others may see it as a challenge to authority.

Culture also influences how young people interpret feedback. Some cultures prefer direct communication, while others value more indirect, subtle cues. Tone, gestures, and phrasing all carry different meanings depending on cultural influences. This makes it important for adults to be mindful of these nuances when speaking with young people.

Cultural sensitivity is an essential factor. In an increasingly diverse world, addressing race, gender, and identity within communication practices promotes inclusivity. Recognizing these elements prevents misunderstandings and strengthens relationships with young people. Youth from collectivist cultures may respond better to group recognition, while those from individualistic cultures may value personal achievements (Triandis, 1995). Being aware of these cultural differences helps ensure that our interactions resonate rather than alienate. The goal is to foster an environment where all young people feel valued and motivated to grow.

Communication and Youth Mental Health

The link between communication and mental health can't be overstated. Positive communication builds self-confidence and resilience, while dismissive or negative interactions can contribute to anxiety and self-doubt. Active listening, empathy, and adapting communication styles to align with youth preferences creates an environment where young people feel heard and valued.

Social and Emotional Factors in Communication

Education and media significantly shape how young people process information. Teachers, school environments, and curriculum design impact communication skills, while media, especially influencers and celebrities, affect language, trends, and social norms. It's no secret that a viral TikTok challenge can sometimes carry more weight than a well-intentioned conversation from an adult.

Another powerful social influence is peer relationships. Adolescents are highly attuned to the opinions and behaviors of their friends and social groups. Research shows that peer influence strongly shapes decision-making, often more than parental guidance during teenage years (Brown & Larson, 2009). If a message is in line with their peer group's values, adolescents are more likely to accept it, while anything that contradicts those norms the youth may ignore or reject it. Adults can improve communication by framing messages in ways that feel relevant to the social world of youth rather than presenting them in a way that feels out of touch.

Snapchatter-Tweeta-Talk

Communicating with young people can sometimes feel like speaking an entirely different language. It's a language filled with emojis, TikTok references, and unspoken social rules. Several key factors shape how youth interpret messages, and understanding these influences can help adults communicate more effectively.

Social media and technology have dramatically reshaped how young people engage with language and communication. Research shows that digital communication alters language processing and social interactions because youth tend to rely on shorthand, memes, and emojis to express emotions (Carr, 2020). They may struggle with interpreting nonverbal cues in face-to-face interaction because so many of their interactions happen through screens. A simple period at the end of a text can be perceived as passive-aggressive; at the same time, a brief response may seem dismissive. With these dynamics at work, adults have to adapt their communication styles to be more direct and engaging.

Conclusion

Many intergenerational conflicts originate from communication breakdowns. Baby Boomers, Generation X, Millennials, and Generation Z each have distinct experiences that shape their approach to communication. Effective communication and relationship building requires active listening, open dialogue, and a willingness to adapt.

These same needs apply to parents and teachers; what worked with past generations may not be effective today. As communication styles evolve alongside cultural and technological shifts, modeling mutual respect becomes even more important. Today's youth are digital natives; they have grown up in a world where smartphones, social media, and instant messaging dominate their interactions. Let's also not forget the sheer nature of language is ever-evolving. Slang changes faster than most of us can keep up. What was "lit" yesterday might be "cringe" today. (And if you don't know what that means, you're proving the point.) Generational dynamics can complicate the conversation even further so staying in touch with these linguistic shifts is one of the keys to bridging generational communication gaps.

The key is to acknowledge these influences without dismissing them. By understanding how youth engage, adults can adjust their communication to be more relevant and impactful. Ultimately, effective communication with young people requires an awareness of how their world shapes their perceptions and choices.

By understanding their cognitive development, cultural and social influences, and media habits, adults can relay messages that are more likely to be received with openness and understanding. Rather than trying to imitate youth culture, the key is to communicate authentically, with clarity and respect because nothing makes a young person tune out faster than an out-of-touch attempt at "relating."

NONVERBAL COMMUNICATION

Let's be honest, most times what we say isn't nearly as important as how we say it. Nonverbal communication, the unspoken language of facial expressions, gestures, body language, eye contact, and tone of voice, can either reinforce or contradict our words. It's the secret ingredient in understanding emotions and intentions. Think of it as the background music in a movie: It sets the tone, whether we realize it or not.

Here's where things get tricky. The way adults interpret nonverbal communication may not always align with how kids perceive it or mean it. What we see as a neutral expression might feel like an intense glare to them. With the rise of technology and screen-based interactions, face-to-face communication has become somewhat of a lost art, making it difficult for people, especially young people, to interpret and use nonverbal cues effectively (Turkle, 2015).

Cultural Differences in Nonverbal Communication

Just when you think you've mastered nonverbal cues, cultural differences throw in a plot twist. What's seen as respectful in one culture can be considered rude in another. As mentioned earlier, eye contact is a great example of this dynamic. In many Western cultures, maintaining eye contact is a sign of confidence and attentiveness. However, in some cultures, direct eye contact with authority figures can be viewed as disrespectful (Hall, 1976). This means that before assuming a child is being rude by avoiding eye contact, we have to consider their cultural norms. It's not about taking things personally; it's about listening beyond our own biases.

Gender Norms and Nonverbal Communication

Society has long dictated different expectations for how boys and girls should express themselves. Boys are often encouraged to be assertive, leading to more dominant body language, while girls are expected to be more nurturing, resulting in softer gestures. What is the downside to this? Girls who are assertive may be labeled as aggressive, while boys who display vulnerability may be perceived as weak (Bem, 1981).

Facial expressions are also shaped by gender expectations. Many boys are discouraged from displaying emotions other than anger or general excitement and happiness, while girls are expected to be expressive and warm. In a world where all of us have to be able to interact and get along, how does this impact the outcome? The outcome is a communication gap and inability to express genuine emotion that follows us into adulthood. Understanding these norms allows us to challenge them and create more inclusive spaces for youth expression that isn't diluted by gender biases.

Bridging the Nonverbal Communication Gap

Recognizing the impact of technology, culture, and gender norms on nonverbal cues is essential in strengthening our relationships with youth. By making small adjustments in how we communicate both verbally and nonverbally, we can bridge the gap and develop deeper connections.

Social media and texting have made conflict resolution even trickier than the complications that already exist in the process. Without tone, facial expressions, or context, messages can be misread, leading to unnecessary drama (Turkle, 2015). People also tend to be bolder behind a screen than in person.

If we want young people to develop healthy communication skills, we have to model them ourselves. Whether through nonverbal communication or conflict resolution, our interactions shape their future behaviors. Let's be the example they need, not just the authority they tolerate.

Nonverbal Communication During Conflict

Have you ever noticed how body language shifts during a disagreement? When tensions rise, so do defensive gestures. As adults, our nonverbal behavior during conflict directly influences how youth learn to handle disagreements. If we model self-regulation and open communication, they're more likely to mirror those behaviors. If we cross our arms, roll our eyes, or use aggressive hand gestures, guess what? They'll do the same.

NAVIGATING MODERN COMMUNICATION CHALLENGES

Technology and the Challenge of Digital Communication

The digital age has revolutionized communication, but it has also made connecting with youth more complicated. Social media, texting, and instant messaging have created new avenues for expression, but they've also introduced new barriers to meaningful interaction. Nonverbal cues, tone, and intent often get lost in translation, leading to misinterpretations, misunderstandings, and the occasional emoji-related disaster.

Social media validation or measuring likes, shares, and comments, has become an important factor in the emotional well-being of many young people. While a well-timed "LOL" can diffuse a conflict, digital communication can also pour fuel on the fire of feelings, insecurities, and social anxieties that tend to already dominate the age group. As adults, we have to navigate these spaces carefully. It's far better to be laughed at for being "old and out of touch" than to accidentally use a meme that means something completely different than we thought.

Communication and Digital Interaction

Body language, facial expressions, and gestures can either reinforce a message or create unintended misunderstandings. For today's youth, digital communication adds another layer of complexity. Social media platforms like TikTok, Snapchat, and Instagram influence not only how they talk but also what they talk about and how they perceive themselves and others. Understanding these digital spaces helps those of us in older generations communicate more effectively. Instead of dismissing social media as a distraction, recognizing its role in youth interactions allows for better engagement and connection. It's not about speaking their language fluently but about showing a willingness to try and understand it.

Technology and Nonverbal Communication

With texting, social media, and video calls becoming the primary modes of communication, nonverbal cues are evolving. Emojis have taken over facial expressions, and a simple "like" often replaces an actual nod of approval. While these digital tools offer new ways to communicate, they also reduce opportunities for young people to develop real-life nonverbal skills (Goleman, 2006).

Have you ever sent a text that was misinterpreted? Without tone and facial expressions, messages can easily be misunderstood. This is why teaching young people how to balance digital and face-to-face communication is important. Who remembers the early days of COVID and the awkwardness of video calls? We've all experienced those moments when someone speaks but their mic is muted, or when facial expressions don't quite match what's being said. We don't even need to discuss the times when people didn't realize they could be seen on camera!

Navigating Feedback in the Digital Age

In today's world, feedback isn't limited to face-to-face conversations. It happens through texts, social media, and online learning platforms. Research shows that digital feedback, whether from teachers, peers, or social media interactions, can significantly impact self-esteem and motivation (Turkle, 2015).

Public praise on social media can boost confidence and reinforce positive behaviors, but public criticism can have lasting negative effects. Digital feedback is often permanent and easily misinterpreted without tone and context. Utilizing private, constructive feedback with youth while reserving public praise for genuine accomplishments helps maintain self-esteem and promotes healthier communication.

In an era of constant digital information, media literacy also plays a major role in how youth interpret messages. Young people are exposed to large amounts of content daily, from news and advertisements to social media influencers and entertainment. According to Hobbs (2018), youth are developing increasingly sophisticated skills in detecting inauthenticity and bias in media. If they sense that a message is manipulative or insincere, they are more likely to reject it. This makes transparency and honesty really important when communicating with young people; if they feel they are being "sold" or forced into an idea, they will in fact resist.

Finally, branding and advertising have a significant impact on how messages land with our young people. Companies invest millions of dollars in creating messages that appeal to youthful people by using relatable language, vibrant visuals, and influencers they admire (Kotler et al., 2019). If a message is dull, outdated, or too formal, it risks being ignored entirely. Adults hoping to connect with young people should consider how they present their messages, and make sure that the content is engaging and relevant without feeling forced.

If you're still sending lengthy emails to a generation that thrives on emojis and memes, it might be time to adapt. Understanding and utilizing the communication modalities and styles that are relevant with young people now, texting, social media, or face-to-face chats, can increase receivability. It's not about abandoning your style but about finding a productive blend.

CREATING A SAFE SPACE

Communicating with today's youth requires more than just speaking, it requires intentional listening, trust-building, and an environment where they feel seen, heard, and valued. Adults assume that young people will open up when they're ready. Spoiler alert, many young people don't ever feel safe enough to do that naturally. Creating a safe space for communication isn't just about their emotional well-being, it's about their overall development.

What Exactly Is a Safe Space?

A safe space is more than a room with cozy chairs and motivational posters. (Although let's be honest, who doesn't love a good "Hang in there" puppy poster?) It's an emotional and psychological environment where people feel protected from judgment, rejection, or ridicule. It's a space where individuals can explore their thoughts without fear of being dismissed or criticized for saying the "wrong" thing. Without a safe space for communication and growth, many young people will choose silence, emotional suppression, or the ever-popular *"I'm fine"* while clearly not being fine. These habits can lead to increased anxiety, isolation, and avoidance behaviors that impact their academic, social, and personal lives (Brown, 2018). Teaching nonviolent communication (NVC), which is really just a complicated, technical way to say "talking without blaming people," can help youth move through life's situations more constructively (Goleman, 2006).

Safe Space at Home: Where Trust Begins

If there's one thing every young person needs, it's a safe place to find rest, and home should be that place. It should not just be a place that's safe from the world outside, but emotionally safe on the inside as well. Home should be a space where feelings aren't ignored, questions aren't punished, and honesty isn't met with sarcasm or shame. You can have all the love in the world for your child, but if your tone feels like a threat or your presence is unpredictable, they'll choose silence every time. So what should it be?

An emotionally safe home doesn't mean letting kids say or do anything without correction. It means correction is done with care, and it means mistakes are treated like teachable moments, not character flaws. It means the adults in the room model how to be vulnerable, showing young people how to say things like "I was wrong," "I overreacted," or "Help me understand what you're going through." Modeling this type of healthy communication in the home isn't a sign of weakness; they're signals of safety that our kids and young people are emotionally safe to grow.

Many kids live under a roof where they're clothed, fed, and reminded how much they're loved, yet still feel emotionally unsafe. Why? Because safety isn't just communicated through what's said, but more importantly how it's said and what actions accompany the words.

Creating this kind of space starts with daily habits: checking in without an agenda, allowing silence without forcing a response, and being consistent in both our presence and behavior. Emotional safety doesn't happen overnight, but it grows or diminishes with each moment and interaction. If young people know home is a safe place emotionally, they're more likely to navigate the rest of life with honesty, resilience, and trust.

Listening Is More Than Just Waiting for Your Turn to Talk

Effective communication is a two-way street. Unfortunately, some adults are driving the wrong direction with the windows up. Many young people feel that adults listen just long enough to prepare their next TED Talk, and they're not wrong. Active listening demands patience, restraint, and genuine curiosity. It means putting down the phone (even when it's an important work call), making eye contact, and avoiding the urge to jump in with a "back in my day" anecdote. It requires reflecting back what they've said to ensure that you've genuinely heard them, and validating their emotions, even the ones that you disagree with or that seem minor. What's important to them is important to them regardless if it's important to us. Let's face it, whether we can do it ourselves or even like it, that TikTok dance *is* a big deal when you're fifteen (Gordon, 2020).

Inclusivity: More Than a Buzzword

Let's get one thing straight: If your version of "everyone is welcome here" comes with an asterisk, it's not really a welcoming space. A safe space has to be inclusive, embracing all backgrounds, identities, and experiences. People in general express that they feel alienated when they don't see themselves represented in a space. Mose people, even as adults, fear judgment based on race, gender, sexuality, or personal struggles. Remember how much harder it was to feel confident when we were younger, so if a young person can't see themselves in the room, they'll assume the room wasn't built or intended for them. This means that adults have to set the tone by creating an atmosphere of acceptance that proactively addresses biases, encourages diverse perspectives, and normalizes differences rather than treating them as exceptions (Sue, 2019). Adults have to check their own biases at the door and get comfortable being uncomfortable. Yes, it's work. No, it's not optional. The goal isn't perfection, the goal is progress.

Why Boundaries Build Emotional Security

Contrary to popular belief, creating a safe space is not the same as creating a free-for-all. Boundaries create security, they're not about control. They're about creating predictability in an unpredictable world. Young people need clear expectations for appropriate communication and conflict resolution. When they know what's expected, respectful language, active listening, no interruptions, they tend to feel more secure and conversations are more productive. These aren't rigid rules; they're relational guardrails that help conversations stay constructive rather than turning into verbal dodgeball matches (Steinberg, 2021). Ground rules also give adults a way to model consistency, which is something that, shockingly enough, teenagers don't hate when it's done right. Establishing ground rules like taking turns speaking, avoiding personal attacks, and actually listening helps encourage a culture of mutual respect that promotes openness rather than fear of conflict (Steinberg, 2021).

Trust: The Currency of Connection

You can't fake trust. You can try, but young people have a built-in BS detector that's more sensitive than a car alarm. Trust is built over time and earned through consistent actions, not empty promises. Trust is the foundation of any safe space, and confidentiality is a huge element of that. Young people need to know that what they share won't be broadcast like the latest school gossip. If a student opens up and suddenly hears their story making the rounds like the morning announcements, good luck getting them or anyone else to share again. Make the rules clear up front: What is said in the room stays in the room . . . unless someone's safety is at risk. Transparency builds trust; secrecy and gossip destroy it (Erikson, 1968). When young people see that their privacy is respected, they become more likely to be open about the struggles they're experiencing that they might not share elsewhere (Erikson, 1968). This isn't just for school staff or counselors, young people don't want their worst moments floating the family or church either. Everything they do isn't everyone's business. What if they went around telling everyone what you do behind closed doors?

Creating Spaces Where Honesty Doesn't Feel Risky

Many young people hesitate to express themselves because of fear of being judged; they are incredibly perceptive. They notice tone, side-eyes, and especially the "I can't believe you just said that" look. The minute they sense judgment, the conversation shuts down like a laptop with a dead battery. Adults can counteract this by modeling vulnerability and honesty. This means admitting we don't have all the answers, owning our mistakes, and occasionally sharing our own growing pains to show we're not perfect.

Sharing personal experiences of struggle, growth, and learning (when appropriate) can make it easier for them to relate. Using open-ended questions instead of yes/no prompts can invite deeper conversation and self-reflection during those hard moments and encourage the conversation rather than providing a quick answer that gives them an easy out (Rogers, 1951).

Tackling Difficult Conversations Like a Pro

Difficult conversation topics like mental health, relationships, identity, and societal pressures are inevitable. These topics can sometimes be emotional land mines, but ignoring these topics doesn't make them go away, in fact they tend to grow. Instead, adults should challenge themselves to create a space where these discussions happen naturally, with sensitivity and patience. It's okay to not have all the answers, but it's not okay to pretend the questions don't exist.

Creating a space where these conversations happen naturally and where youth know they can speak their truth without fear of being shut down, leads to connection and healing. Sometimes, the best thing an adult can say is: "I don't have the perfect words right now, but I'm here, and I care" (Kessler, 2019).

Stopping Bullying Before It Silences Voices

A safe space is only as secure as its ability to protect those within it. You can't call a space "safe" if bullying is quietly thriving in the background like mold in a forgotten Tupperware. Bullying, whether overt or subtle, can quickly turn a welcoming environment into one filled with fear and self-doubt. Leaders have to take a proactive approach and ensure that negative behaviors aren't tolerated. The consequences should be clear, but so should opportunities for learning and reconciliation. Creating a proactive stance means not just punishing the behavior once it happens, but also educating young people ahead of time about its impact and giving space for restoration and growth if it occurs (Olweus, 1993).

Digital Spaces: The New Frontier of Communication and Chaos

In case anyone missed the memo: Communication has officially gone digital, and it's not going backward. Group chats, private stories, and ten-second video clips are where young people now do their most "authentic" talking. Digital spaces are their comfort zones, confession booths, battlefields, and unfortunately, sometimes their bullies' playgrounds. We have to responsibly acknowledge that with great connectivity comes great risk and responsibility.

These platforms are fertile ground for cyberbullying, misinformation, fear of missing out (FOMO)–induced anxiety, and the threat of screenshots living forever in someone's camera roll. Teaching digital responsibility and safety isn't just a tech lesson, it's a social-emotional one. Adults are challenged with helping young people understand that every like, post, and direct message (DM) carries weight. Privacy settings are not foolproof, and "deleting" doesn't always mean it's gone. We have to help our young people realize that viral moment they're chasing might not be the kind of fame they'll want in five years (Boyd, 2014). The bottom line is they need safe digital spaces too; ones shaped by respect, awareness, and maybe just a pinch less drama.

Turning Conversations into Tangible Support

A safe space shouldn't just be a place to vent, it should also be a bridge to solutions. Many young people don't know where to turn when they need help. Listening is a great start, but it can't be the end-all. A safe space has to come with an exit plan for when talking isn't enough. Some young people need more than encouragement; they need access: to mental health professionals, school counselors, social workers, mentors, safe adults, and peer-led groups. Our young people need an actual safety net, not just the well-meaning sentiment of saying "I'm here for you."

When an adult tells a young person, "You should talk to someone," it isn't helpful if no one is available or if the "someone" is booked until next semester. Schools, communities, and programs have to make sure young people don't just hear about support but see it, have access to it, and trust it. All of these elements are foundational in creating safe spaces that are more than just suggestion boxes with great ideas and no follow-through (Noddings, 2012). Providing access to mental health professionals, peer support groups, mentorship programs, and other resources ensures that when our words aren't enough, there are tangible next steps (Noddings, 2012).

Why Relationships Matter More Than Reassurances

Relationships are the backbone of effective communication. When young people feel a connection with the adults and peers around them, they are more likely to engage in meaningful conversation. Consistency is one of the keys to building this connection. Showing up, being present, and proving yourself to be reliable over time shows our young people that we are committed to being there for them.

It's not enough to say, "You can talk to me anytime." That phrase sounds nice, but let's be real, most young people aren't walking through that door if they're not sure what's behind it. Relationships are the real key. This type of relationship isn't about friendliness, it's not about being "the cool adult," but it's the kind of relationship that's built through consistency, care, and credibility. Show up. Be present. Follow through. Those aren't just leadership strategies, they're how trust is built brick by brick.

Young people don't always test us with words; they test us with silence, side-eyes, and missed assignments. How we respond to those subtle signals says everything. "My door is open" becomes meaningful only when students believe that we'll meet them where they are, even if they never walk all the way in (Pianta, 1999).

Creative Expression: When Words Just Aren't Enough

Not everyone is comfortable expressing themselves through conversation. For some youth, "Tell me how you're feeling" feels like a pop quiz they didn't study for. Not everyone has the words or the courage to verbally articulate what they're going through. That's where creative outlets come in like art, music, dance, journaling, photography, poetry, or even meme-making (yes, memes). We have to change our perception of these outlets and realize that these aren't distractions, they're vehicles.

Expression doesn't have to be grammatically correct to be emotionally profound. Providing tools and time for creative expression in safe spaces opens the door for reflection and release, especially for young people who don't engage well through the traditional conversation. If a poem or freestyle rap helps a young person say what they couldn't in a sit-down chat, mission accomplished (Csikszentmihalyi, 1996).

Respecting Autonomy in Every Interaction: "Good Intentions" Aren't a Free Pass

Respecting personal boundaries is so incredibly important. This could mean asking before offering advice, making sure there's comfort before discussing sensitive topics, or asking permission before sharing someone's story. Consent creates an environment where young people feel in control of their own path (Freire, 1970). Sometimes adults swoop in with advice, storytelling, and "life lessons" before the young person even finishes their sentence. It's not usually malicious, but as adults, we have to realize that it's often just muscle memory. The issue is that intent doesn't cancel out impact, or lack of impact. Without consent, even well-meaning advice can feel intrusive. Not everyone gives your advice the credibility that you think it deserves.

Asking for permission, "Is it okay if I offer a thought?" or "Would you like support, or just someone to listen?", models respect. It also gives the young person control over their narrative. Consent builds trust and it shows that we don't assume their story belongs to us just because we're in the room (Freire, 1970). In a world where so many decisions are made *for* our young people, that moment of choice matters.

Letting Youth Lead the Spaces Meant for Them

One of the best ways to create a safe space is to give young people ownership of it. Allowing them to take leadership roles like peer mentoring, organizing discussions, or having a voice in the rules, reinforces that the space belongs to them. When youth have a voice in shaping their environment, they engage more deeply and hold each other accountable (Zeldin, 2004). It's not about handing over the keys and walking away. It's about co-creating something meaningful with them in the driver's seat and us navigating from the passenger side. This teaches accountability in a way that sticks. Youth-led spaces tend to hold higher expectations for behavior, inclusiveness, and follow-through than adult-led ones because the buy-in is real. They want the space to succeed because it reflects them, not just someone else's program binder (Zeldin, 2004).

Keeping Safe Spaces Dynamic and Evolving

Let's face it, no matter how great a space feels today, if nothing changes, it starts to feel stale. Growth is the fuel that keeps safe spaces relevant. Regular feedback (the honest kind, not just "It was fine") from the youth themselves helps adults stay responsive. What worked for a group of fifteen-year-olds last year may not work for this year's group.

Change isn't failure, it's evolution, and being open to change means being open to critique. Anonymous suggestion boxes, post-meeting check-ins, and group evaluations are all examples of ways to shape and reshape their safe space without fear of hurting feelings or stepping on toes (Brookfield, 1995). Flexibility is the name of the game, because if we don't grow with them, they'll outgrow our usefulness.

Closing Thoughts: Safe Doesn't Mean Silent

Creating a safe space for youth communication isn't a one and done effort, it's an ongoing commitment to understanding, empathy, and trust. When young people feel safe to express themselves without fear of judgment, they develop the tools to navigate their emotions and experiences. It's not about being perfect, it's about being present. It's about recognizing that young people don't need us to fix them, but they do need us to show up, truly listen, and provide a space where their voices aren't just allowed but honored. When we support them in developing these skills, we empower them to communicate effectively and grow into confident, self-aware adults who know their voices matter and how to use them.

When young people feel safe emotionally, physically and socially, they start to trust. When they trust, they talk, and when they talk, we get the privilege of walking alongside them in the beautiful, complicated journey of becoming. That's the work, and that's the mission. Yes, it can be messy, but it's also where the magic happens.

WHEN COMMUNICATION
BREAKS DOWN

Even with our best efforts, there will be times when communication falls apart. Sometimes, despite all the nodding, paraphrasing, and well-intentioned advice, we just can't get on the same page; conflict is inevitable. It's as much a part of life as taxes and Wi-Fi issues. The key is to recognize that these moments are normal.

The real danger isn't in the occasional miscommunication, it's in how we react to it. When frustration takes over, conversations often shift from understanding to defensiveness. The disconnect that people feel is rarely personal, yet we often take it that way. Instead of allowing frustration to strain the relationship, we should focus on identifying the true cause of the feeling(s) and put that in its proper perspective. Is it that we disagree with what's being said? Are we disappointed in what has happened? No matter what the reason, identifying the source of the frustration is critical toward controlling our response to it. If we can master doing this, we can avoid some of the impact that would come with the conflict and instead build trust and offer the support young people need (Siegel, 2012).

Take a quiet, yet honest moment of reflection and think about how you respond when things don't go your way or work out the way you had hoped they would. Do you start using your one mouth more than your two ears? Does your volume increase? How about that body language part that we talked about earlier? How we model conflict resolution is important because, whether we like it or not, kids are watching. More often than not, they won't do as we say, they'll do as we do (Bandura, 1977).

Agreeing to Disagree

When we talk about disagreement, I think it's important to start right here. Not every disagreement needs a winner. Learning to respect differences instead of pushing for a right-or-wrong outcome creates a number of possible positive outcomes. Let's also take a heartfelt moment right now and agree to retire the phrase "because I said so." It doesn't build trust; it just shuts down conversation. Now let's talk about what happens when conflicts or disagreements do occur.

Navigating Conflicts with Empathy and Understanding

Effective communication during disagreements requires empathy and a commitment to understanding the other person's perspective. It means actively listening to the other person, acknowledging their feelings, and addressing the underlying issues rather than just the surface argument. Often, young people present a smoke screen of argument that distracts our focus, but the responsibility of control and maintaining the healthiness of the conversation lies on us as adults.

By keeping focus on what's important, hearing what they're trying to say, ask, or tell us, we can reduce the tension. This means letting go of our side of the tension over whatever the issue is because we understand that their frustration is not even likely about us. Sometimes the argument is the only way that they know how to ask for help. How we respond will reinforce that they can either talk to us or not. A controlled, positive response during a disagreement can help young people feel heard, respected, and valued way faster than peace times. When we prioritize empathy, we model for young people how to handle their emotions and disagreements in a constructive way and teach them that conflicts can be resolved without resentment or anger, and even if those things happen, apology and reconciliation are okay too.

Communication Techniques in Conflict

During conflicts, certain communication techniques can be more effective than others. Techniques like using "I" statements allow individuals to express their feelings without playing the blame game and can prevent the other person from becoming defensive. For example, saying, "I feel overwhelmed when chores aren't done because it adds to my workload," is more constructive than accusing someone of never doing chores or calling them lazy. Asking clarifying questions will help to make sure there's clear understanding and shows a genuine interest in the other person's viewpoint. These strategies are respectful and provide a model for young people to copy.

Setting Boundaries in Disagreements

Setting clear boundaries is very important in managing conflicts. This means understanding and communicating your limits and tolerances. Clearly defining what's acceptable and what's not helps prevent misunderstandings and sets the foundation for healthy interactions. For young people, learning to set and respect boundaries is an important life skill that will help improve their personal and professional relationships in the long-term.

The Role of Forgiveness and Moving Forward

Forgiveness plays an undervalued role in resolving conflicts and maintaining relationships and communication. Teaching young people the importance of forgiveness, letting go of grudges, and not holding past wrongs against someone helps them develop resilience and emotional maturity. It encourages a forward-looking approach. It pushes them to focus on what they can learn from the experience rather than dwelling on the conflict itself, which they can't change. Giving appropriate importance to forgiveness helps to strengthen relationships because it shows young people that they can encounter a challenge and still recognize the importance of preserving relationships.

Peer Support: An Opportunity for Growth

Peer mediation programs empower young people to resolve conflicts themselves. These can be school based, community based, or even within the home. They simply require the modeling then empowering of young people to interact in healthy ways with support, empathy, and tolerance. We have to understand that sometimes young people will simply make mistakes and that's okay. These approaches, no matter the environment, model healthy communication and equip young people with skills they can carry into adulthood.

Creating Opportunities for Positive Outcomes

Every conflict presents an opportunity for growth and learning. When disagreements are handled constructively, they can lead to a deeper understanding between the people involved. This can improve problem-solving skills and lead to healthier communication overall. When adults turn conflicts into learning opportunities, we empower young people to handle future issues more effectively and more independently. We equip them with the tools to navigate other situations and relationships throughout their lives with greater healthiness and happiness.

The Journey to Becoming a Better Communicator

One of the hardest realities that I've had to accept in this process is that I used to be a terrible communicator. Once I accepted this truth, I started seeing this same problem everywhere. Most of us were never explicitly taught what healthy communication looks like. Instead, we learned to suppress emotions, avoid hard topics, and shut down when conversations became uncomfortable. We model this behavior for our kids, yet we expect them to do better.

How do you know if you're a healthy communicator? Look at how you interact with other adults. Do you yell? Then your child probably will, too. Do you bottle up emotions? Your child is watching and learning. Are you a poor listener? Don't be surprised when they follow suit. If we want our kids to be better communicators, we have to lead by example. This means embracing uncomfortable conversations, practicing active listening, and showing emotional vulnerability.

RESEARCH-BASED SUGGESTIONS FOR EFFECTIVE, HEALTHY COMMUNICATION

The Art of Effective Communication

If communication were as easy or as simple as talking, the majority of us would be experts. Real communication, however, especially with young people, requires more than just words. It requires active listening, trust-building, and an awareness of how modern technology influences the way our youth interact. Young people crave connection, but they will only engage authentically if they feel safe, respected, and valued (Brown, 2018).

The Power of Role Modeling in Emotional Development: They Do as We Do, Not as We Say

When it comes to teaching young people how to handle their emotions, the most important practice, yet the one that's almost always overlooked, is role modeling. We spend a lot of time telling kids to "express their feelings" and "communicate openly," yet so many of us forget to model these behaviors ourselves. It's like handing someone a car with no driving lessons and expecting them to navigate rush-hour traffic. If we want young people to develop healthy emotional coping skills, we need to show them what that looks like in how we act, react, and interact.

It's a hard truth, but one worth repeating: Kids don't just listen to what we say; they mirror what we do. No matter how many heartfelt talks or bedtime prayers we throw their way, they are far more likely to imitate our actions than our words. Research consistently supports the truth that kids adopt the emotional regulation strategies they observe in their caregivers (Bandura, 1977).

Give yourself a few minutes to reflect on your own habits once again. What have you been teaching the young people in your life?

If a child grows up watching their role model(s) bottle up stress, lash out in anger, or avoid difficult conversations, they are more likely to do those exact same things and use those same coping mechanisms. On the flip side, when they see adults practice self-awareness, resilience, and openness in their communication, they learn that expressing emotions is not just acceptable, it's healthy and desirable. We are all walking, talking emotional instruction manuals for the next generation. The question is, What kind of manual are you writing?

Building Trust Through Consistency

Trust isn't built overnight; it's earned through repeated actions. It's not enough to say, "You can talk to me anytime." They need to see that your support is consistent and reliable. If a young person opens up about something vulnerable and we respond with impatience, dismissal, or punishment, they'll definitely think twice about doing it again (Siegel & Bryson, 2016).

Consistency also means modeling the behaviors we encourage or expect. If we ask young people to communicate openly, we have to be willing to consistently do the same around them and with them. This doesn't necessarily mean oversharing personal struggles, but rather demonstrating emotional honesty in a way that reinforces mutual trust appropriately and regularly. Hard times and feelings aren't a one-time thing in life. We have to teach our young people that in each of these situations or circumstances, it's okay to express how they feel and that they can both seek and trust the adults around them to hear and support them.

Why Empathy and Perspective-Taking Matter

Let's be honest, communicating with young people can sometimes feel like trying to decipher a foreign language. Between the new yearly slang, changing social norms, and the occasional eye roll, making a genuine connection can be hard. In spite of the difficulty, one universal truth remains: Empathy and perspective-taking are game-changers for opening up meaningful communication.

Empathy is the ability to understand and share in another person's feelings. It helps create an environment of trust where young people feel safe expressing themselves. When adults validate a youth's emotions and show compassion, they break down barriers and create deeper connections (Goleman, 2006).

Perspective-taking is the ability to see the world through another person's eyes. By intentionally considering a person's experiences and viewpoints, we can relate better to their struggles, aspirations, and daily realities. Do you remember being a kid? Do you remember being a teenager? You don't have to remember everything to remember it was hard. Drawing on those memories will allow you a chance to take a step back and relate better. When we can relate, we can understand, and when we can understand, we can connect.

The Power of Empathy in Building Trust

Empathy is the bridge that allows us to truly connect with young people. Validating their emotions builds trust and creates an environment where they feel safe enough to authentically express themselves. The issue is that everything gets tested when difficult conversations arise.

Empathy is the core of strong relationships. When young people feel heard and understood, they are more likely to allow us in. Empathy also helps improve communication by allowing adults the ability to consider their approach in ways that genuinely connect with the young people around them. It's a powerful tool for de-escalating conflicts because acknowledging emotions can simmer down defensiveness and open the door for opportunities for resolution (Rogers, 1951). Beyond our topic of communication, displaying empathy supports emotional well-being. It has been shown to help young people feel valued and less isolated.

Teaching youth to communicate effectively during emotionally charged situations is a challenge, but it's a necessary skill. Active listening, validating emotions, and maintaining a calm demeanor are essential techniques for modeling healthy emotional regulation; the key word is *modeling*. When young people learn to manage their emotions in a healthy way, they increase their EI and overall well-being (Brackett, Rivers & Salovey, 2011).

For some people, empathy comes naturally. For others, it is a skill that requires a conscious effort. Either way, intentional practice makes a difference. Emotional tone can often matter more than the words themselves when speaking to young people. Studies show that adolescents are particularly sensitive to tone and body language, sometimes perceiving neutral statements as negative due to heightened emotional processing (Somerville, 2013). Young people can dismiss even the best advice if it comes across as judgmental, dismissive, or condescending. They may shut down in response to a critical tone but engage more openly with messages delivered in a supportive or humorous way. Keeping conversations calm, respectful, and engaging can make a significant difference in how young people receive them. We have to remember that if our message or support is worth giving, then it's worth giving in a way that others can receive it.

Developing Empathy and Perspective-Taking

There are a few strategies that will help to improve our ability to show empathy and perspective-taking, but it all starts with active listening. Imagine you're a detective in a classic mystery novel. Before jumping to conclusions, you gather clues. Taking the time to truly listen to young people allows us to understand their perspectives and concerns. Active listening not only builds trust but also ensures your responses are relevant and meaningful. Remember, it's not about waiting for your turn to speak; it's about clearing your thoughts and allowing your only focus to be their narrative, then to be able to provide an appropriate response . . . if needed.

Maintaining eye contact, responding with thoughtful affirmations, and avoiding interruptions all help support deeper, more meaningful conversations. Validating emotions, sometimes with something as simple as "That sounds tough," can reassure young people that their feelings are being heard and understood.

Modeling empathy and perspective-taking in everyday interactions holds the biggest weight in connecting and communicating with our youth. Young people almost always learn more from observing behavior than from being told what to do. Showing patience, owning mistakes, and being understanding sets an example they are likely to follow (Bandura, 1977).

Open-Ended Questions Encourage Conversation: Being Curious Not Judgmental

If you've ever asked a teenager, "How was your day?" and received a one-word reply of "Fine," you know the struggle. Open-ended questions are the kryptonite to conversation dead ends like this. Open-ended questioning pushes for a deeper response and encourages meaningful conversation (Goleman, D. 2006). Talking about and asking them about their interests, whether it's a favorite show, a video game, or a school event, shows them that their world matters.

Teenagers often feel like they're starring in their own reality show, complete with drama and their own thoughts and reflections. By displaying a genuine interest and curiosity of their experiences and emotions, you show empathy and create a comfortable and safe space for openness. Phrases like

"I understand that this is important to you" can bridge the generational gap and make them feel seen.

Adults have to embrace adaptability, empathy, and curiosity if they want to bridge generational gaps. Communication with youth isn't just about delivering information and directions, it's about building trust and understanding. Instead of handing them the answers on a silver platter, pose questions that stimulate their thinking and problem-solving.

Encouraging young people to assess information empowers them and strengthens their decision-making skills. It's like teaching them to learn to fish and allows them the skill of inquiry in their future rather than giving them a fish and maintaining their dependence on others to solve their problems. Teaching them to fish for wisdom is a skill that can never be taken away and often eliminates some of the battles that come when we simply provide information and direction. Self-discovery and determining our own direction are huge motivators toward better and more informed conversations and interactions.

The magic of an open-ended question lies in its ability to unlock more than just surface-level answers; it opens up trust, emotion, and often, a whole story waiting to be told. Unlike closed questions that invite a quick yes or no (or worse, a one-syllable grunt), open-ended questions show a desire to understand, not just to check a box. The best ones usually begin with "what" or "how." For example, instead of the standard "Did you have a good day?", which is basically asking for a polite lie, try something like, "What was the most challenging part of your day?" or "How did you feel about what happened at lunch?" These questions signal that we're not just making small talk, we're actually interested in the full picture.

Once you ask the question, the next challenge is often . . . silence. Embracing the pause is critical. Silence can feel uncomfortable for adults who are used to filling in every gap in conversation like they're hosting a live radio show, but for young people, that pause might be the space they need to gather their thoughts, sort their feelings, or decide if they're ready to trust you with the truth. Give them that moment. Sit with it and resist the urge to rescue the silence with a follow-up joke or mansplained clarification.

When the conversation starts to unfold, encourage them to go further. Follow-ups like "Can you tell me more about that?" or "What do you think would help next time?" show genuine curiosity, not interrogation. These small nudges invite deeper reflection and remind young people that their voice matters, not just their answer. The goal isn't to extract information like an emotional detective, but to build a dialogue that highlights their experience.

The power of open-ended questions isn't just in the words we use, it's in the message they send: that we care more about understanding than about being right. When young people sense that their ideas and emotions aren't just being tolerated but valued, they're far more likely to engage in real, honest, and meaningful conversations.

Effective Feedback and Praise: Striking the Right Balance

Young people thrive on feedback when it's done right. Effective feedback is specific, behavior-focused, and encouraging. Instead of vague praise like "Good job," offering feedback like, "I really liked how you explained your thinking on that math problem" provides more genuine, specific reinforcement. Feedback should also highlight areas of improvement while also recognizing accomplishments, celebrating a sense of progress rather than perfection (Hattie & Timperley, 2007). Practice makes progress.

Research shows that constructive feedback enhances self-awareness, self-regulation, and motivation. When young people understand both their strengths and areas they can improve, they are more likely to take ownership of their growth and develop resilience.

The Role of Praise in Motivation

Genuine praise boosts confidence and encourages perseverance. Too much praise or poorly delivered praise can be counterproductive. Over-the-top, ingenuine compliments like "You're the best student ever!" feel as insincere as they are meant. It's also important that our praise encourages a growth mindset. For example, focusing solely on intelligence rather than effort can create a fixed mindset instead of motivation to grow and progress (Dweck, 2006).

The most effective praise highlights effort and progress rather than just outcomes. Recognizing hard work reinforces a growth mindset, where young people see challenges as opportunities rather than intimidating threats. Finding the right balance between praise and feedback helps them develop a strong sense of self-worth, confidence, and motivation.

The Role of Feedback and Praise in Education

Teachers play an important role in shaping students' academic mindsets. Effective classroom feedback is timely, actionable, and goal oriented; it helps students monitor their own progress. Praise in educational settings should also focus on effort, persistence, and problem-solving strategies, reinforcing that success comes from hard work rather than fixed intelligence.

Parental involvement is key. When parents and educators provide consistent feedback and praise, young people develop a positive academic identity and become resilient in their learning.

Cultural Sensitivity and Communication

Many intergenerational conflicts come from communication breakdowns. For effective communication and relationship-building to coexist, active listening, open dialogue, and a willingness to adapt are required. These same needs apply even deeper to parenting; what worked with past generations may not be effective today. As parenting styles evolve alongside cultural and technological shifts, creating environments of mutual respect becomes even more important.

Culture influences how young people interpret feedback. Some cultures prefer direct communication, while others value more indirect, subtle cues. Youth from collectivist cultures may respond better to group recognition, while those from individualistic cultures may value personal achievements (Triandis, 1995).

Being aware of these cultural differences helps ensure that praise and feedback encourage rather than alienate. The goal is to develop environments where all young people feel valued and motivated to grow.

Cultural Responsiveness in Feedback and Praise

Cultural sensitivity is another essential factor in effective communication. In an increasingly diverse world, addressing race, gender, and identity within communication practices promotes inclusivity. Recognizing these nuances prevents misunderstandings and strengthens relationships with young people.

Research shows that constructive feedback enhances self-awareness, self-regulation, and motivation. When young people understand both their strengths and areas for improvement, they are more likely to take ownership of their growth and develop resilience.

Cultural Awareness: Inclusivity and Fairness

The role that cultural awareness plays is significant in developing quality communication and relationships with young people. Cultural backgrounds shape how young people express emotions and interpret feedback and influence how they communicate and respond to adults. It's almost impossible to understand every difference and culture that we see in our world today, so how do we navigate the slippery slope that culture brings to this hope for improved communication and relationship? It's important to make sure that our interactions are fair, inclusive, and free from unconscious bias (Hall, 1976). This means realizing that the way we were raised in comparison to how another was raised is not a debate of right or wrong, but simply a matter of difference.

Humor or Hurtful?

Humor can be the secret sauce that makes conversation more engaging. It's important, however, to use it cautiously and carefully. A well-timed, light-hearted joke can ease tension, but sarcasm or humor at someone's expense can backfire. Think of humor as a spice: The right amount enhances the dish, but too much spice or applying it to the wrong dish can ruin it.

Setting Boundaries and Establishing Rules

One of the greatest challenges in communicating with young people is setting boundaries. While rules provide structure, boundaries define acceptable behaviors. When you communicate boundaries and rules clearly, you reduce confusion, establish trust, and enhance emotional well-being.

Enforcing boundaries, however, isn't always easy, especially in the digital age. Peer pressure, social media, and ever-changing societal norms all influence how young people respond to rules. Adults have to be flexible in order to find balance, while also figuring out how to maintain their core values.

Effective Strategies for Setting Boundaries

Setting boundaries is an essential part of fostering healthy relationships with young people. One of the most effective strategies is active listening, which involves giving the speaker your full and undivided attention. When young people feel heard and their emotions are validated, they are more likely to trust and respect the boundaries being set. This approach helps reassure them that their thoughts, feelings, and perspectives matter, and it creates space for an open line of communication.

Another effective method is collaborative decision-making, where youth are actively involved in establishing rules. Allowing them to have a say in the process increases their sense of responsibility and ownership over the boundaries in place. When young people feel included, they are more likely to follow the expected rules because they see them as fair and necessary rather than forced upon them.

Equally important is explaining the "why" behind rules and expectations. Giving young people a clear reason helps them understand the purpose of the boundary. In turn, this makes them more likely to cooperate. When young people see that rules are not random, but rather put in place to ensure their well-being, they are more likely to respect and follow them.

Consistency and fairness are critical factors in maintaining effective boundaries. Enforcing rules in a predictable and equitable way encourages stability and trust. When young people know what to expect and see that consequences are applied fairly, they feel secure and are less likely to push back.

In today's digital age, setting digital boundaries is extremely important. Establishing guidelines for technology use, including screen time limits and appropriate online behavior, helps make sure that young people engage with digital platforms in a safe and responsible manner. Adults can help young people navigate the digital world by setting clear expectations for internet use, social media interactions, and online safety. By using these strategies, we can create a structured, supportive environment where young people understand and respect boundaries, leading to healthier relationships and personal growth. Schools and families that prioritize clear communication and boundary-setting typically see benefits.

Active Listening: The Secret Weapon

Active listening is more than just hearing words; it's the commitment to truly understanding, responding, and remembering what is being said. In today's fast-paced, tech-saturated world, genuine listening has become a rare skill, but it's more critical than ever.

Active listening encourages trust and respect. When young people feel heard, they are more likely to open up and share their thoughts, experiences, and emotions. This deepens relationships and creates opportunities for mentoring and guidance (Rogers & Farson, 1987).

Active listening is not a passive skill, it's a deliberate practice that helps reassure young people that their voices matter. It's the difference between merely hearing words and truly engaging with someone's thoughts and feelings. Here are a few strategies to enhance active listening:

1. Practice patience—Let them express their thoughts fully and don't interrupt, even if you disagree from the first sentence.
2. Show empathy—Put yourself in their shoes (even if those shoes are trendy sneakers that cost more than your entire wardrobe).

3. Use nonverbal cues—Maintain eye contact, nod, and offer encouraging gestures to show you're paying attention.

4. Provide feedback—Paraphrase what they've said to confirm your understanding and validate their feelings.

5. Ask open-ended questions—Encourage dialogue rather than shutting down conversations. Avoid questions with simple yes/no, two-option responses.

6. Minimize distractions—Put down the phone, turn off notifications, and be fully present.

7. Paraphrase and summarize—Reflecting their thoughts back to them validates their feelings and encourages further discussion. An example statement of this would be, "It sounds like you're frustrated because you don't feel heard, have I understood what you're expressing correctly?"

8. Suspend judgment—If a young person shares something difficult, resist the urge to react with criticism. Instead, respond with curiosity and empathy: "That sounds tough, what do you think would help you in this situation?"

9. Maintain eye contact—This signals attentiveness and shows that you're fully present. But be mindful, this is not a creepy, unblinking stare that makes them wonder if you're buffering, but rather attentiveness and eye contact when they're speaking.

10. Avoid interruptions—Jumping in with solutions before they've finished speaking can make young people feel unheard. Sometimes, they just need to vent, not receive a five-step action plan.

Body Language: The Silent Messenger

The way we carry ourselves sends a message before we even open our mouths. Youth pick up on body language cues more than we realize, and they're surprisingly good at decoding whether an adult is authentically engaged or just tolerating the conversation. To help make things simple, let's categorize body language into two areas: positive (open) body language and negative (closed) body language:

Positive Body Language Habits

- Eye contact—Not the creepy, unblinking kind, just enough to show attentiveness.
- Upright posture—Because slouching screams "I'd rather be anywhere else."
- Smiling or a neutral facial expression—A simple smile goes a long way.

- Authentic gestures of acknowledgment—A well-timed nod can do wonders.
- Open body stance—Uncrossed arms and relaxed shoulders signal approachability.

Negative Body Language Habits

- Lack of eye contact—A classic sign of distraction or discomfort.
- Crossed arms—The universal pose of defensiveness.
- Fidgeting—Restless movements often indicate anxiety or impatience.
- Negative facial expressions—Frowning, grimacing, or looking generally annoyed.
- Lip biting and eye rolling—Both communicate frustration or dismissal.
- Poor posture—Slouching can indicate disengagement.
- Exaggerated gestures—Over-the-top movements can come across as aggressive.
- Hands on hips—The classic "I'm not mad, I'm just disappointed" stance.
- Looking at a watch or phone—The universal signal that you're over it.

If you notice, the negative list is longer. That's because negative body language is often unconscious, which makes it hard to control. Awareness is an important first step in improving our nonverbal communication, especially with our young people.

Understanding the Digital Landscape

We've discussed already that in today's world, communication isn't limited to face-to-face conversations. Social media, texting, and online forums have become the primary spaces where young people express themselves. While these platforms provide opportunities for connection, they also open the door to risks such as cyberbullying, misinformation, and privacy concerns (Twenge, 2017). Adults have to acknowledge and discuss these digital realities so we can help guide our young people in navigating online interactions responsibly. Conversations about emotional well-being should extend to how social media impacts self-esteem, relationships, and overall mental health.

Ethical Considerations in Communication

Respecting privacy, autonomy, and transparency encourages ethical communication. This matters even for your own kids. Youth need to feel safe, valued, and heard. When these basic respectful factors guide interactions, relationships flourish, and communication becomes a tool for empowerment rather than control.

Conclusion: The Commitment to Better Conversations

Communication with our youth is ever evolving; it requires effort to understand the filters that influence and impact their ability to hear. When adults prioritize connection over correction, they build stronger, more meaningful relationships. This helps ensure that messages not only reach young people but truly resonate with them.

Mastering active listening, utilizing open-ended questioning, building trust through consistency, and understanding technology's impact are crucial factors in developing meaningful connections with young people. The goal isn't to perfect a script but rather to nurture a mindset of adaptability and empathy. We have to remember that the most powerful lesson we can offer is the example we set.

Creating an emotionally healthy society starts with us when we model resilience, practice open communication, and show that vulnerability is not a weakness, but rather a strength. When we do this, we empower the next generation to express themselves with confidence, seek help when they need it, and know how to navigate their emotions in a way that leads to growth rather than suppression. The bottom line is if we want young people to learn how to handle life's challenges, we have to show them how it's done. No pressure, right?

CONCLUSION:
LET'S TALK—AND KEEP TALKING

As we close the pages of *Let's Talk: Communicating with Today's Youth*, it's important to remember that this is not the end of the conversation, it's the beginning of a new way of showing up. We don't need to be perfect communicators, flawless listeners, or emotion-decoding experts to make a difference. What we do need is the courage to try. We need the courage to be intentional and to lean into moments of discomfort with grace and determination. The reality is, if we don't, we risk losing the very connection that could change the direction of a young person's life.

The data is clear that young people who feel heard and emotionally supported are significantly more likely to succeed academically, socially, and emotionally (Goleman, 1995; CASEL, 2020). Emotional intelligence, especially in adults, has been shown to predict more effective parenting, teaching, and mentoring outcomes. On the flip side, when youth experience dismissiveness, judgment, or emotional neglect in their interactions, it can contribute to increased rates of anxiety, depression, and risky behavior (Siegel, 2012). This isn't just about getting teens to open up, it's about unlocking their potential by creating a culture of trust and consistency.

Finding our way with better communication starts with small shifts. Asking "What made you feel proud today?" instead of "Did you have a good day?" Choosing to pause and sit in silence rather than fill the air with assumptions. Offering validation rather than correction when a young person shares their frustration. These are not difficult acts, but they are deliberate ones, and in a world that moves too fast and listens too little, deliberate communication is a radical act of love.

Adults have to take the lead in this work; young people learn more from what we model than what we mandate (Bandura, 1977). If we want emotionally intelligent, communicative, and resilient young people, then we have to first become emotionally intelligent, communicative, and resilient adults. This is not a passive hope, it is an urgent call to action. There is no policy or program that can replace the power of a consistent, present adult who knows how to ask the right questions, listen deeply, and respond without judgment.

If we rise to the occasion, we can create a generation that not only feels understood but knows how to understand others. That ripple effect doesn't just impact classrooms and living rooms, it reshapes communities. If we remain passive, if we continue to rely on outdated "because I said so" methods or hide behind digital distractions, we risk further alienating a generation already shouting to be heard in a dangerous world full of noise.

So let's talk, but more than that, let's *listen*, let's *learn*, and let's lead by example. The stakes are too high, and the opportunity is too great. This isn't just about improving communication, this is about saving relationships, embracing futures, and creating a world where every young person knows they matter. They are watching us. Let's give them something worth imitating.

REFERENCES

Arnett, J. J. (2015). *Emerging adulthood: The winding road from the late teens through the twenties* (2nd ed.). Oxford University Press.

Bandura, A. (1977). *Social learning theory*. Prentice Hall.

Bem, S. L. (1981). Gender schema theory: A cognitive account of sex typing. *Psychological Review, 88*(4), 354–364.

Brackett, M. A., Rivers, S. E., & Salovey, P. (2011). Emotional intelligence: Implications for personal, social, academic, and workplace success. *Social and Personality Psychology Compass, 5*(1), 88–103.

Boyd, D. (2014). *It's complicated: The social lives of networked teens*. Yale University Press.

Brookfield, S. D. (1995). *Becoming a critically reflective teacher*. Jossey-Bass.

Brown, B. (2018). *Dare to lead: Brave work. Tough conversations. Whole hearts*. Random House.

Brown, B. B., & Larson, R. W. (2009). Peer relationships in adolescence. In R. M. Lerner & L. Steinberg (Eds.), *Handbook of adolescent psychology* (pp. 74–103). Wiley.

Carr, N. (2020). *The shallows: What the internet is doing to our brains*. W. W. Norton & Company.

CASEL. (2020). *What is SEL?* Collaborative for Academic, Social, and Emotional Learning. https://schoolguide.casel.org/what-is-sel/what-is-sel/

Chapman, G., White, P., & Myra, J. (2007). *The 5 languages of appreciation in the workplace: Empowering organizations by encouraging people*. Northfield Publishing.

Csikszentmihalyi, M. (1996). *Creativity: Flow and the psychology of discovery and invention*. Harper Perennial.

Dweck, C. S. (2006). *Mindset: The new psychology of success*. Random House.

Erikson, E. H. (1968). *Identity: Youth and crisis*. Norton.

Farrel, B., & Farrel, P. (2017). *Men are like waffles, women are like spaghetti: Understanding and delighting in your differences*. Harvest House Publishers.

Freire, P. (1970). *Pedagogy of the oppressed*. Bloomsbury.

41

George, J. M. (2000). Emotions and leadership: The role of emotional intelligence. *Human Relations, 53*(8), 1027–1055.

Goleman, D. (1995). *Emotional intelligence: Why it can matter more than IQ.* Bantam Books.

Goleman, D. (2006). *Social intelligence: The new science of human relationships.* Bantam.

Gordon, T. (2020). *Parent effectiveness training: The proven program for raising responsible children.* Three Rivers Press.

Gross, J. J. (1998). The emerging field of emotion regulation: An integrative review. *Review of General Psychology, 2*(3), 271–299.

Gross, J. J., & John, O. P. (2003). Individual differences in two emotion regulation processes: implications for affect, relationships, and well-being. *Journal of Personality and Social Psychology, 85*(2), 348–362. https://doi.org/10.1037/0022-3514.85.2.348

Hall, E. T. (1976). *Beyond culture.* Anchor Books.

Hattie, J., & Timperley, H. (2007). The power of feedback. *Review of Educational Research, 77*(1), 81–112.

Hobbs, R. (2018). *Mind over media: Propaganda education for a digital age.* W. W. Norton & Company.

Kessler, R. (2019). *The needs of the spirit in learning and teaching.* ASCD.

Kotler, P., Kartajaya, H., & Setiawan, I. (2019). *Marketing 4.0: Moving from traditional to digital.* Wiley.

Noddings, N. (2012). *The ethics of care: Personal, political, and global.* University of California Press.

Olweus, D. (1993). *Bullying at school: What we know and what we can do.* Wiley-Blackwell.

Pianta, R. C. (1999). *Enhancing relationships between children and teachers.* American Psychological Association.

Rogers, C. R. (1951). *Client-centered therapy: Its current practice, implications, and theory.* Houghton Mifflin.

Rogers, C. R., & Farson, R. E. (1987). Active listening. In R. G. Newman, M. A. Danzinger, & M. Cohen (Eds.), *Communications in business today* (pp. 61–72). Heath.

Salovey, P., & Mayer, J. D. (1990). Emotional intelligence. *Imagination, Cognition and Personality, 9*(3), 185–211.

Santrock, J. W. (2021). *Children* (14th ed.). McGraw-Hill.

Siegel, D. J. (2012). *The whole-brain child: 12 revolutionary strategies to nurture your child's developing mind.* Bantam.

Siegel, D. J., & Bryson, T. P. (2016). *The developing mind: How relationships and the brain interact to shape who we are* (2nd ed.). Guilford Press.

Somerville, L. H. (2013). The teenage brain: Sensitivity to social evaluation. *Current Directions in Psychological Science, 22*(2), 121–127.

Steinberg, L. (2014). *Age of opportunity: Lessons from the new science of adolescence.* Houghton Mifflin Harcourt.

Steinberg, L. (2021). *Adolescence.* McGraw-Hill.

Sue, D. W. (2019). *Microaggressions in everyday life: Race, gender, and sexual orientation.* Wiley.

Ting-Toomey, S., & Dorjee, T. (2018). *Communicating across cultures.* Guilford Press.

Triandis, H. C. (1995). *Individualism & collectivism.* Westview Press.

Turkle, S. (2015). *Reclaiming conversation: The power of talk in a digital age.* Penguin.

Twenge, J. M. (2017). *iGen: Why today's super-connected kids are growing up less rebellious, more tolerant, less happy—and completely unprepared for adulthood.* Atria Books.

Zeldin, T. (2004). *Conversation: How talk can change our lives.* HiddenSpring.

Select portions of this manuscript were supported by AI-assisted tools to enhance clarity, structure, and stylistic consistency. All core ideas, insights, and conclusions remain solely those of the author.

DISCUSSION QUESTIONS

1. Why is it so hard to talk to kids today? What are some reasons parents and kids struggle to understand each other, and what can parents do to make conversations easier and more meaningful?

2. How do feelings affect the way we talk? How can parents and kids better recognize emotions in themselves and each other to have more positive conversations?

3. Are parents really listening? What does it mean to truly listen to a child, and how can parents show they are paying attention in a way that makes kids feel heard?

4. Can body language say more than words? How might a parent's facial expressions or tone of voice affect what a child hears? Can these nonverbal signals help or hurt communication?

5. Why do small arguments turn into big fights? What are some simple ways parents and kids can handle disagreements without yelling or shutting down?

6. Do kids and parents see the world the same way? How might a parent's childhood be different from a child's life today, and how does that change the way they communicate?

7. What messages do kids really hear? If parents think they are giving good advice, why do kids sometimes feel misunderstood? How can parents adjust the way they explain things so kids truly understand?

8. Is technology helping or hurting family conversations? How does social media and texting change the way kids and parents talk to each other? What are some ways families can balance technology and real conversations?

ACTIVITIES TO SUPPORT IMPROVED COMMUNICATION

1. Topic: Active Listening TechniquesActivity: Practice active listening with your child by engaging in a conversation where you demonstrate techniques like summarizing, clarifying, and asking open-ended questions.

2. Topic: Understanding Emotions and Their Impact on Communication Activity: Create an emotions chart together with your child, identifying different emotions and discussing how they can affect communication. Share personal experiences and brainstorm strategies for managing emotions during conversations.

3. Topic: Conflict Resolution Strategies for Parents and Children Activity: Role-play various conflict scenarios with your child, taking turns as the parent and child. Practice effective communication techniques such as using "I" statements, finding compromises, and active problem-solving.

4. Topic: Power of Praise and Effective Feedback Activity: Write down three specific instances where you can provide genuine praise to your child. Discuss the impact of positive reinforcement and practice giving constructive feedback by focusing on behavior rather than personal attributes.

5. Topic: Communicating Across Cultures and Generations Activity: Research different cultural communication norms and traditions together. Share insights and discuss ways to bridge any communication gaps that may arise due to cultural or generational differences.

6. Topic: Setting Clear Boundaries and Rules Activity: Collaborate with your child to establish family rules and boundaries. Discuss the reasoning behind each rule and create a visual representation, such as a family contract or poster, to serve as a reminder.

7. Topic: Role-playing Exercises for Effective Communication Activity: Create role-playing scenarios based on common communication challenges. Take turns playing the parent and child, practicing effective communication techniques learned throughout the workbook.

8. Topic: Journaling Prompts for Self-Reflection and Growth Activity: Provide journaling prompts for parents to reflect on their communication experiences, emotions, and challenges. Encourage regular journaling to track progress and identify areas for improvement.

9. Topic: Real-Life Scenarios to Practice New Communication Skills Activity: Present real-life scenarios where effective communication is crucial, such as conflicts with friends or homework struggles. Work through these scenarios with your child, applying the communication strategies discussed in the book.

10. Topic: Recap and Ongoing Improvement Activity: Write a personal reflection on the progress made throughout the book and identify specific goals for ongoing improvement in parent-child communication. Create a visual reminder, such as a vision board or affirmation cards, to stay motivated.